NEW VANGUARD 334

TANKS IN THE PHILIPPINES 1944–45

The biggest armored clashes of the Pacific War

STEVEN J. ZALOGA   ILLUSTRATED BY FELIPE RODRÍGUEZ

OSPREY PUBLISHING

Bloomsbury Publishing Plc

Kemp House, Chawley Park, Cumnor Hill, Oxford OX2 9PH, UK

29 Earlsfort Terrace, Dublin 2, Ireland

1385 Broadway, 5th Floor, New York, NY 10018, USA

E-mail: info@ospreypublishing.com

www.ospreypublishing.com

OSPREY is a trademark of Osprey Publishing Ltd

First published in Great Britain in 2024

A catalog record for this book is available from the British Library.

ISBN: PB 9781472859402; eBook 9781472859426;
ePDF 9781472859433; XML: 9781472859419

24 25 26 27 28   10 9 8 7 6 5 4 3 2 1

Index by Fionbar Lyons

Typeset by PDQ Digital Media Solutions, Bungay, UK
Printed by Repro India Ltd.

Osprey Publishing supports the Woodland Trust, the UK's leading woodland
conservation charity.

To find out more about our authors and books visit
www.ospreypublishing.com. Here you will find extracts, author
interviews, details of forthcoming events and the option to sign up for our
newsletter.

Title page image: see caption on p. 26

CONTENTS

TANKS IN THE PHILIPPINES 1944–45

The biggest armored clashes of the Pacific War

INTRODUCTION

The campaign in the Philippines involved the largest tank operations by either side in the Pacific War. It marked the first and only time that the Japanese Army committed one of its few armored divisions against US forces. The 2nd Tank Division was fielded on Luzon, while Japanese forces on neighboring Leyte included several tank companies. On the US side, the campaign included the deployment of seven tank battalions, three tank destroyer battalions, and a separate tank company, totaling over 500 tanks and tank destroyers.

Tanks had been used extensively by both sides in the first Philippines campaign of 1941–42. The Japanese invasion force included two tank regiments that played a prominent role in spearheading the advance by the Imperial Japanese Army (IJA). The US Army fielded the Provisional Tank Group on Luzon with two light tank battalions and a self-propelled tank destroyer battalion.

Tank operations in the Philippines were heavily dependent on the terrain. Many of the islands consist of forested mountains unsuitable for any type of mechanized operation. The main island of Luzon has a large plain that was the principal battlefield for tank operations both in 1941–42 and again in 1945. The terrain elsewhere usually restricted large-scale tank operations by either side. However, tanks often proved invaluable in providing mobile fire support for the infantry, even in these challenging circumstances.

A pair of Type 97-kai Shinhoto Chi-Ha of the 10th Tank Regiment knocked out during the fighting between the Harada Group of the IJA 2nd Armored Division and the 25th Division near San Isidro.

DOCTRINE AND ORGANIZATION

IJA doctrine and organization

Japanese tank organization and doctrine were heavily shaped by the experiences of the war in China since 1937. The IJA decided to form tank divisions in the wake of its defeat at Nomonhan in Manchuria against the Red Army in 1939. The plan was to create ten armored divisions to serve as a counterweight to Soviet military power. Following the German victory over France in

One of the late-production Type 89 Yi-Go Ko medium tanks of the 7th Ind. Company knocked out on the road near Jualita on Leyte on October 22, 1944 during the fighting with the 184th Infantry.

1940, a delegation headed by Gen Tomoyuki Yamashita toured Germany to study the lessons of the recent European fighting. The Yamashita report recommended deeper mechanization of the IJA. The IJA organized three armored divisions in Manchuria in the summer of 1942 and a fourth was created in Japan in July 1944. The organization of additional armored divisions was prevented by decisions in Tokyo in 1942.

In the wake of the successful Pacific offensive that started in December 1941, Tokyo was forced to make a strategic shift. The focus on the China/Manchuria theater shifted to the defense of Japan's newly acquired conquests in the Pacific. This led to severe cuts in Japanese tank development and production in favor of warships and aircraft. The value of tank units in defending the new Pacific island conquests was open to question. The fighting in the Solomons and elsewhere in the Southwest Pacific in 1942–44 clearly demonstrated the limited value of tanks in mountainous and jungled terrain.

In the summer of 1944, the Imperial General Headquarters (IGHQ) decided to transfer the 2nd Armored Division from the Kwangtung Army to Luzon for the defense of the Philippines. Luzon was the only plausible site for its deployment since the other large islands were mountainous with few areas suitable for tank employment. By the time that the 2nd Armored Division was deployed in September 1944, it had been trimmed back in size due to the transfer of several of its units to other theaters. Further losses were suffered when its convoys heading to the Philippines were attacked.

The commander of the 14th Area Army in the Philippines was the same Gen Yamashita who had recommended the creation of the armored divisions in 1940. He had subsequently displayed considerable acumen in his use of tanks in the 1941–42 Malaya campaign. By 1944, Yamashita was skeptical of the value of the armored divisions in the defense of the Philippines. The original plans envisioned using the 2nd Armored Division as a counterattack force to wage a decisive battle on the Central Plains of Luzon against American forces landing in the Lingayen Gulf. However, the brisk destruction of Japanese tank units in the Marianas and Peleliu in the summer of 1944 raised doubts in Yamashita's mind whether the 2nd Armored Division had the technical effectiveness to prevail in a direct confrontation against the much more powerful American Sherman tanks.

Tank strength of IJA 2nd Armored Division on Luzon

Unit	Type 97 medium	Type 95 light	Other AFVs
Divisional HQ	7	2	-
3rd Tank Brigade HQ	6	5	2
6th Tank Regiment	57	9	1
7th Tank Regiment	55	17	-
10th Tank Regiment	55	4	1
2nd Mobile Infantry Regiment	-	-	9
2nd Mobile Artillery Regiment	-	-	2
2nd Engineer Regiment	-	-	24
Divisional Maintenance	17	-	-
Total	**197**	**37**	**39**

Besides the 2nd Armored Division, the IJA deployed several independent tank companies to the Philippines. Three of these were equipped with the old Type 89 Yi-Go medium tank, the 7th Tank Company on Leyte and the 8th and 9th Tank Companies on Luzon. Two light tank companies equipped with the Type 95 Ha-Go light tank were broken off the 2nd Armored Division for defense on Leyte. The Imperial Japanese Navy's (IJN) Special Naval Landing Force had their own Type 2 Ka-Mi amphibious tanks and these were used in a landing on Leyte in December 1944 as detailed below.

US Army doctrine and organization

The US Army deployed about a third of its separate tank battalions to the Pacific Theater of Operations (PTO) in World War II; none of its armored divisions were deployed to the PTO. Although the US Army had focused on the use of tanks for infantry support in the 1930s, the formation of the Armored Force in 1940 led to an accent on the armored divisions and their operational mission of deep exploitation. Separate tank battalions were relatively small in number until 1943 when the reorganization of the armored divisions freed up over 30 battalions. In addition to new tank battalions formed in 1943, this expanded the US Army from 27 to 70 separate tank battalions by the end of 1943.

Company A, 775th Tank Battalion in the fields south of Baguio, Luzon, on March 8, 1945 while supporting the 123rd Infantry, 33rd Division. Co. A used dice insignia as seen here. The tank in the foreground was named "Angel Puss" after a Looney Tunes cartoon feature released in the summer of 1944.

Ignoring for a moment the use of two tank battalions in the Philippines in 1941–42, the US Army had very limited experience in the use of tanks in the Pacific until 1944. The jungle-covered mountains of the Southwest Pacific were not well suited to tanks. The first extensive combat use by the US Army was in the Solomons, Dutch New Guinea, Hollandia, and the Marshall Islands in early 1944. These operations usually involved very small numbers of tanks, often only a company or less. The larger islands of the Central Pacific provided better terrain for tank operations. Both the Marine Corps and US Army employed tanks in battalion strength in the Marianas and Palau Islands in the summer and early fall of 1944.

Aside from the difficulties of local terrain and weather, the main tactical problem was tank–infantry cooperation. The Army Ground Forces Headquarters issued a directive in April 1943 that stressed the need for more combined training by tank and infantry units. However, the lack of joint training was an acute problem in the Pacific since infantry divisions were often thousands of miles away from the tank battalions assigned to support them during forthcoming operations. For example, during the Leyte operation, only one tank battalion and infantry division were co-located on the same island prior to the operation. A post-war study of armor operations in the Pacific described this key tactical problem:

A direct result of this lack of training was a feeling of distrust between the [infantry and armor]. It evolved from a misunderstanding of each other's capabilities and limitations. Infantry commanders felt that the tanks were not sufficiently aggressive when they wouldn't push blindly out in the face of the enemy who had stopped the foot soldiers. In return, the tank felt that when the going got stiff and the lead started flying, the infantryman would desert him. If the tanker couldn't see the accompanying infantry, he immediately surmised that he had been abandoned not realizing that in the close underbrush, the infantryman was still there but had merely crouched down to avoid being a larger target. This situation was further aggravated by the lack of tank-infantry communications and the whole business became a major problem when the weather, heat, and mud increased. It finally straightened itself out as the tankers and infantrymen became used to each other and learned expensively to be sure just what each could, would, and was prepared to do in support of each other. By the end of the campaign, the tank-infantry team was pretty well coordinated and bound together by mutual trust and respect.

The need for close tank–infantry cooperation was especially critical in the Pacific theater due to Japanese infantry anti-tank tactics. Due to a shortage of anti-tank (AT) guns or specialized anti-tank weapons comparable to the US Army's 2.36in bazooka rocket launcher, Japanese anti-tank tactics focused on the use of close-range suicide attacks using satchel charges. Japanese teams would conceal themselves along likely avenues of tank approaches, and then leap out and hurl the satchel charge onto the engine deck of the US tank.

"Battle Baby," an M4 of Lt Jack Baltz, commander of the 1st Platoon, Co. B, 775th Tank Battalion, is guided up a narrow mountain road on the Villa Verde Trail on Luzon on April 3, 1945.

This type of attack could be thwarted by accompanying US infantry, but it required constant and close cooperation between the infantry and tanks.

Tank battalions in the Pacific seldom operated as a complete unit but were usually divided into companies to support different infantry regiments during operations. The most common role for tank companies in the Philippines was direct fire support of infantry units to clear out Japanese strongpoints that had otherwise resisted attack. These were typically machine gun nests or defenses built into buildings of field fortifications. When terrain was too poor to permit tank

use, tank companies could be attached to divisional artillery to serve in the artillery support role using indirect fire.

The amphibious tank battalions had their own set of tactics due to their unique vehicles. The LVT(A)1 and LVT(A)4 amtanks (amphibious tanks) were weakly armored. As a result, their primary mission was to provide fire support while swimming ashore during the initial phase of amphibious landings. Their tactics on reaching shore were constrained by their vulnerability to Japanese heavy machine guns and other weapons due to their thin hull armor. In many cases, the LVT(A)4 were then attached to the divisional artillery for indirect fire missions. During the island fighting, amtanks were sometimes used as mini-gun boats. They would enter the water near a Japanese strongpoint and then bombard it from offshore while the infantry assaulted it from land. In some cases, amphibious tank battalions and amphibious tractor battalions would form task forces to conduct small-scale amphibious landings on smaller islands. By the time of the Philippines campaign, army amphibious tank battalions had a mixture of both the LVT(A)1 and LVT(A)4.

Tank destroyer battalions were used in small numbers in the Pacific theater. These were usually the self-propelled battalions equipped with the M10 3in Gun Motor Carriage (GMC) or M18 76mm GMC, not the towed battalions with the M5 3in gun. These tank destroyer battalions were used in much the same fashion as tank battalions for direct fire support of the infantry or attachment to divisional artillery for indirect fire.

One distinct difference in the Pacific theater from the European theater was the use of assault guns and self-propelled howitzers in lieu of towed howitzers in the infantry regimental cannon companies. These companies usually had three platoons, each with two cannon for a total of six 75mm or 105mm howitzers per regiment. In the Pacific in 1944, the M8 75mm Howitzer Motor Carriage (HMC) assault gun or the M7 105mm HMC were substituted for the towed cannon. These self-propelled guns were usually used in the direct fire role like tanks rather than in the indirect fire role. In some cases, regimental anti-tank companies had M10 3in GMC tank destroyers substituted for towed AT guns.

TECHNICAL FACTORS

Japanese tanks and AFVs

The predominant Japanese tank in the Philippines was the Type 97-kai Shinhoto Chi-Ha. This was an improved version of the original Type 97 Chi-Ha but with a new turret fitted with a 47mm high-velocity gun instead of the low-velocity 57mm gun fitted on the original version. Development of the 47mm gun had begun in 1939 in response to Japanese experiences fighting the Soviet Army in Manchuria. This was intended for the new Type 1 medium tank that also had thicker frontal armor to offer protection against the Soviet 45mm gun.

Armor penetration, Japanese 47mm vs US 75mm guns

(vertical armor)	500yds	1,000yds
Japanese 47mm APHE (mm)	67mm	55mm
US 75mm M61 APC (mm)	74–86mm*	66–79mm*

Difference due to homogenous vs face-hardened plate

The dramatic shift in Japanese industrial policy in 1942 downgraded the priority previously given to tank production. Production of the new Type 1 tank was delayed until 1943, and instead, the interim Type 97-kai Shinhoto Chi-Ha (Shinhoto: new turret) was produced in 1942–43 despite its inadequate armor. This used the new 47mm gun turret, but not the thicker armor or improved engine of the Type 1. A handful of Type 97-kai tanks were rushed to the Philippines in 1942 and took part in the final battle on Corregidor. The Type 97-kai Shinhoto Chi-Ha did not reappear in the Pacific War until the fighting in July 1944 on Saipan and Guam. The Japanese 2nd Armored Division was equipped primarily with the Type 97-kai Shinhoto Chi-Ha since its original mission was to combat the Red Army in Manchuria. A very small portion of its medium tanks were the earlier Type 97 Chi-Ha with the 57mm gun.

The Type 97-kai Shinhoto Chi-Ha was closer in technical features to the US Army's M5A1 light tank than to the M4 medium tank, weighing only about half as much as the M4. Its 47mm gun could not penetrate the frontal armor of the M4 medium tank, though it could penetrate the side armor. Its own armor was vulnerable to frontal penetration by both the American 37mm and 75mm tank guns.

Comparative technical characteristics

	Type 97-kai	M4A3(W)
Combat weight ton/tonne	17.4/15.8	34.8/31.5
Engine	Mitsubishi SA 12200VD	Ford GAA
Horsepower	170	450
Horsepower/weight ratio (HP/ton)	9.7	12.9
Road speed (mph/kmh)	24/38	26/42
Range (miles/km)	130/210	100/160
Ground pressure (psi)	8.7	14.3
Armor		
Turret front	33mm @ 0°	89mm curved
Turret sides	26mm @ 11°	51mm @ 5°
Hull glacis	25mm @ 11°	64mm @ 47°
Lower hull	20mm @ 30°	51–114mm curved
Hull side	26mm @ 25°	38mm @ 0°

A captured Japanese T12 (M3) 75mm GMC tank destroyer that fell off a bridge on Luzon. This was one of at least three US tank destroyers captured from the Provisional Tank Group in 1942 that remained in Japanese service in the 1945 fighting. The Japanese inscription on the side, "Gyo Senryo," is a warning to IJA troops not to fire on it because it has been captured.

The Type 95 Ha-Go light tank was the most widely built Japanese tank of the war with about 2,700 manufactured between 1936 and 1943. Although adequate for its intended missions in the China theater in the late 1930s, it was not well suited to combat in the Pacific War due to its weak armor. However, it was far easier to transport than the medium tanks and so it ended up scattered in small numbers in Japanese garrisons all over the Pacific. The 2nd Armored Division had about 60 of these in service in 1944.

The Philippines campaign was the last stand of the old Type 89 Yi-Go medium tank. About 400 had been built between 1931 and 1939 and they saw extensive combat in China and in the early 1941–42 campaigns in the Pacific. It was armed with a low-velocity 57mm gun and was weakly armored. There were three independent companies of Type 89 medium tanks still in service in 1944 in the Philippines: the 7th Tank Company on Leyte, and the 8th and 9th Companies on Luzon. The IJA in the Philippines still operated several M3 light tanks and T12(M3) 75mm GMC tank destroyers captured from the US Provisional Tank Group in 1941–42. The 2nd Armored Division had a handful of self-propelled guns on Luzon including the Type 1 Ho-Ni armed with the Type 90 75mm gun and the Type 1 Ho-Ro with a Type 38 150mm howitzer. The division also had a variety of other specialized armored vehicles including armored personnel carriers and various types of armored engineer vehicles.

The IJN had its own tank force assigned to the Special Naval Landing Force (SNLF). The IJN sponsored the development of amphibious tanks, the most significant of which was the Type 2 Ka-Mi. They saw their combat debut in small numbers on Kwajalein in February 1944 and on Saipan in July 1944. They were often delivered to the landing beach on a 2nd-class landing

A

JAPANESE TANKS ON LEYTE

1. Type 89 Yi-Go medium tank, 7th Ind. Company, Leyte, October 1944. The 7th Ind. Tank Company on Leyte in 1944 appears to have retained the pre-1942 color scheme, suggesting that these tanks were the same ones used in the 1941–42 campaign in the Philippines. This shows a typical camouflage scheme in the late 1930s consisting of medium brown (*Cha-iro*), mahogany brown (*Tochi-iro*), and dark green (*Midori-iro*) with the yellow disruptive stripe. Some equipment provided to the manufacturer by government arsenals such as the 57mm gun and tools were delivered in khaki primer.

2. Type 95 Ha-Go light tank, 1st Ind. Company, 1st Infantry Division, Leyte, December 1944. The Type 95 tanks on Leyte came from the 2nd Armored Division and were finished in the simplified 1942 scheme. This standard three-color finish consisted of "parched grass" primer corresponding to DIC350 (Dai-Nippon Ink and Chemicals industrial color standard) and roughly corresponding to the Wehrmacht 1943 dark yellow color. This was a rust-preventive paint and was even supposed to be applied over the tracks. The two principal camouflage colors were a dark olive which ranged from a dark olive green to an olive drab shade corresponding to DIC510/ DIC531; and a dark mahogany brown, corresponding to DIC521. No markings were evident on the tanks of this company, though it may have carried the standard regimental marking of the 10th Tank Regiment from which it was detached.

The most potent Japanese armored vehicle from the IJA 2nd Armored Division was the Type 1 Ho-Ni 75mm self-propelled gun, attached to the division's mechanized artillery regiment. This Type 1 Ho-Ni was captured by the US Army's 37th Division near Aritao on April 6, 1945.

ship that could carry five to seven Type 2 Ka-Mi tanks. The Itoh Detachment sent to the Philippines in 1944 originally had 37 Type 2 Ka-Mi tanks.

US Army tanks and AFVs

The predominant US Army tank in the Philippines campaign was the M4 medium tank, popularly called the Sherman. Two variants were most often seen in the Philippines, the M4 (composite) and the M4A3(W). The M4 (composite) was a sub-variant of the M4 version manufactured by Chrysler's Detroit Tank Arsenal from August 1943 through January 1944. These were essentially similar to the standard M4, but employed a new hull that incorporated a cast front superstructure derived from the cast hull of the M4A1; the remainder of the hull was of the normal welded construction.

"Bushmaster," an M4 of Co. B, 763rd Tank Battalion, stuck in soggy ground while providing indirect fire support for the 96th Division near Dagami on Leyte on November 23, 1944. This is a late-production M4 composite hull with the large drivers' hatches.

An M5A1 light tank No. 11 of Co. D, 44th Tank Battalion named "Ginny" during the landing operations near Tacloban on Leyte on October 20, 1944 while supporting the 1st Squadron, 7th Cavalry Regiment, 1st Cavalry Division.

The M4A3(W) was a new version of the M4A3 that incorporated a new welded hull with a reconfigured front superstructure with larger drivers' hatches. A more important feature was the use of "wet" stowage, hence the odd use of the (W) suffix by Ordnance. The wet stowage involved the relocation of the hull ammunition stowage from the sponsons to new floor bins that were surrounded by "wet" compartments to reduce the risk of ammunition fires. The M4 medium tank was twice as heavy as the Japanese Type 97-kai Shinhoto Chi-Ha and could destroy it at normal combat ranges. The Sherman's frontal armor protected it from the Japanese 47mm gun.

US tank battalions in 1944 had three tank companies with M4 medium tanks (Companies A, B, and C) and one company (Company D) with M5A1 light tanks. By 1944, the M5A1 was obsolete. Its 37mm gun was not especially useful in destroying typical Japanese field fortifications and its thin armor was vulnerable to the Japanese 47mm gun. As a result, the M5A1 companies were often given secondary missions to keep them out of harm's way while the M4 medium tanks shouldered the main combat burden. US tank battalions also contained six M4 or M4A3 105mm assault guns. These resembled the normal Sherman tank but had a 105mm howitzer in the turret instead of the usual 75mm gun. These were intended to provide immediate indirect fire support for the other tanks.

The amphibious tank battalions were equipped with the LVT(A)1 and LVT(A)4 amphibious tanks (amtanks). The LVT(A)1 was based on the LVT-2 but fitted with a turret derived from that of the M5A1 light tank. The LVT(A)1 entered production in August 1943 with 328 going to the Army and 182 to the Marine Corps by the time that production ceased in February 1944. These were not especially popular in service since the 37mm gun was not very effective in destroying typical targets during landing operations such as Japanese machine gun bunkers. It was replaced by the LVT(A)4 that substituted the turret from the M8 75mm HMC.

Two types of tank destroyers were used in the Philippines campaign, the M10 3in GMC and the M18 76mm GMC. The tank destroyers were not especially popular in the Pacific theater since their open turrets made the crew vulnerable to ever-present Japanese snipers or close-attack with satchel charges. Tank destroyer doctrine was irrelevant in the Pacific theater, and they were generally used for direct fire support of the infantry, or in a secondary artillery role with indirect fire support to supplement infantry division field artillery.

THE CAMPAIGN

Operation *King-2*: Leyte
Operation *King-2*, the Sixth US Army amphibious landing on Leyte, was the preliminary step in the liberation of the Philippines. The strategic intention was to secure ports and airfields to support the main effort on neighboring Luzon. Leyte's geography was dominated by the extinct volcanoes of the Central Cordillera Range that formed the spine of the island. There were two coastal plains suitable for tank operations. The coast along the northeast corner of the island included the provincial capital of Tacloban as well as the city of Dulag and its nearby airfields. This was the most plausible landing area. To the northwest was the open terrain of Carigara leading into the Leyte peninsula.

At the start of the Leyte campaign, the main Japanese defenses were Lt Gen Shiro Makino's 16th Division. This concentrated on the coastal plains in the northeast of Leyte. The only significant Japanese armor on the island was Capt Kono's 7th Independent (Ind.) Tank Company. It was equipped with 11 old Type 89 medium tanks, probably vehicles that had been deployed in the Philippines in the initial 1941–42 campaign. This company was stationed at Buruaen, ten miles from the coast.

The Japanese Army had originally expected to withhold decisive ground action until the invasion of Luzon. However, the Imperial Japanese Navy mistakenly believed it had crippled the US carrier fleet during the battle of the Taiwan Sea on October 12–16, 1944. As a result, the Imperial General Headquarters decided to throw all available ground strength into Leyte to secure an early decisive victory.

A pair of LVT(A)1 amtanks of the 776th Amphibious Tank Battalion on Red Beach, Leyte, during the landing operation on October 20, 1944.

The Sixth US Army landings consisted of two corps, the X Corps to the north landing near Tacloban, and the XIV Corps to the south near Dulag. The two corps each deployed two infantry divisions, each supported by a separate tank or tank destroyer battalion for armored support.

The preliminary naval bombardment demolished most of the Japanese coastal defenses, so the American landings on October 20, 1944 were not heavily contested in the initial phase. The first waves included the LVT(A)4 amtanks to provide immediate fire support. The tank battalions were landed in later waves. For example, the 767th Tank

Battalion had four platoons in Wave 5 while the remainder of the battalion landed in Waves 10 through 14.

US armor on Leyte 1944

Battalion	Corps	Initial assignment
44th Tank Battalion	X Corps	1st Cavalry Division
706th Tank Battalion	XXIV Corps	77th Division
763rd Tank Battalion	XXIV Corps	96th Division
767th Tank Battalion	XXIV Corps	7th Division
776th Amphibious Tank Battalion	XXIV Corps	7th Division
780th Amphibious Tank Battalion	XXIV Corps	96th Division
632nd Tank Destroyer Battalion	X Corps	24th Division

The Japanese 7th Ind. Tank Company was ordered to counterattack. A few of its tanks encountered the advancing Co. G, 184th Infantry near Jualita, losing one to a rifle grenade. Accompanied by the 20th Infantry Regiment, the rest of the 7th Tank Company launched a night attack around 0130hrs on October 21. After a day of costly fighting with the 184th Infantry, the 7th Ind. Tank Company had lost eight of its 11 tanks. The three remaining tanks were found abandoned near Buruaen due to a blown bridge that prevented further withdrawal.

Once the beachhead was secured, American columns pressed further inland. In the only battalion-sized tank action of the Leyte campaign, the 767th Tank Battalion was assigned along with the 17th Infantry, 7th Division to push west out of the Dulag bridgehead and seize the airfields near Buruaen. The three medium tank companies reached Buruaen by afternoon. Three tanks were disabled, mainly by aircraft bombs buried in the road as mines. Coordination with the infantry was poor and the tanks were isolated two miles ahead with no infantry support. In the late afternoon, the tanks were ordered to return to bivouac since it was policy to position tank units behind the infantry defenses at night. Japanese resistance had been light and it was presumed that it would remain so the following day.

The advance on October 23rd repeated the same mission with admonitions for better coordination. The Japanese had not been idle, and during the night had established anti-tank defenses along the road including mines. The tanks reached Buruaen at 1020hrs, but the advance ground to a halt due to several tanks blocking the road after hitting mines and others becoming stuck in neighboring swamps. The 17th Infantry began to clear the town around noon. The airfields were secured later in the afternoon. The two days of fighting cost the 767th Tank Battalion nine M4 Sherman and three M5A1 light tanks, mainly on the second day. The 7th Division commander, Maj Gen Albert Brown, relieved the tank battalion commander for lack of aggressiveness. The advance on the Buruaen airfields by the 767th Tank

A pair of Type 89 medium tanks of the 7th Ind. Tank Company knocked out on the road near Jualita on Leyte on October 22, 1944 during the fighting with the 184th Infantry.

A pair of M8 75mm HMCs of the 1st Cavalry Division ashore on Leyte on October 21, 1944. By 1944, many infantry regiments in the Pacific theater substituted these assault guns for towed howitzers in their regimental cannon companies.

Battalion was the last time that any of the US Army tank battalions were used on Leyte in a battalion-sized action. This had nothing to do with the controversy over the action, but rather due to the inevitable constraints on tank actions due to the mountainous terrain encountered beyond the beachhead.

Following the American landings, the Imperial General Headquarters ordered the transfer of three divisions to Leyte, the 1st, 26th, and 102nd Divisions. They were landed at the port of Ormoc on the opposite side of Leyte from the American landings. They marched from Ormoc to the Carigara plains northwest of the American beachhead to stymie any further American advance. The reinforcements included only two tank companies since it was felt that Leyte was poorly suited to tank operations. Both were assigned to the IJA 1st Division and reached Leyte in early November. Both tank companies had ten Type 95 light tanks; each were detached from the Japanese 2nd Armored Division on Luzon. After landing on Leyte, these two companies were initially used to drag the artillery and ammunition of the 1st Division up the steep mountain roads toward Limon Pass on the way to the Carigara plains.

B

SHERMANS OF THE 44TH TANK BATTALION

1. M4A1 Composite, Co. A, 44th Tank Battalion, Leyte, October 1944. The 44th Tank Battalion had elaborate markings with each company having its own style. Co. A used horizontal bars to indicate the platoon, so the three bars here indicate 3rd Platoon. This platoon also used a distinctive wolf's-head cartoon. The tank names did not follow the usual army practice of following the company letter, so some of the company names included *Southern Cross*, *Heliza Poppin*, *Bloodthirsty*, *Little Caesar*, and *Lucky's Goldbricks*. Headquarters tanks usually used another symbol rather than the bars.

2. M4A1 Composite, Co. B, 44th Tank Battalion, Santo Tomas University, Manila, February 1945. Co. B used rank chevrons to indicate the platoon, so the three chevrons here represent 3rd Platoon and the number below (1) indicates the tank number. Co. B also used a variety of names, some starting with the company letter but many not following this practice: *Ole Miss*, *Yankee*, *A.P.O. Manila*, *Broadway Terror*, *Heart Breaker*, *Georgia Peach*, *Block Buster*, etc.

1

SOUTHERN CROSS

U.S.A.
3031405

2

OLE MISS

A Type 95 light tank knocked out during the fighting along Highway 2 near Ormoc in December 1944. This tank belonged to either the 1st or 2nd Ind. Tank Companies that were supporting the 1st Division.

The first week of fighting in late October saw the US X Corps advance to the north with an aim to skirt around the mountains via the coastal plains near Carigara. The pace of the land fighting slackened on October 23–26 due to the eruption of a titanic naval battle in the neighboring Leyte Gulf. The naval battle diverted most of the naval gunfire support and air support for several days. The resounding defeat of the Japanese fleet severely complicated the plans of the Imperial General Headquarters to reinforce Leyte since Japanese shipping became extremely vulnerable to American naval and air interdiction.

The Leyte campaign was primarily an infantry battle with tanks playing a supporting role when possible. Once the Sixth US Army had pushed out of the coastal plains of the bridgehead, the terrain turned forested and mountainous. A post-war report commented that "There were many occasions on Leyte when tanks were not used in support of [infantry] operations simply because the commanders felt that the terrain was so prohibitive that they abandoned all hope of keeping the tanks up with the infantry. They frequently gave up hope too easily."

Aside from the difficult terrain, weather played a significant role in restricting the use of tanks. Heavy rain began to fall on November 3; a typhoon arrived November 8, inundating the island through November 17 and severely curtailing tank operations.

Rather than being used in battalion strength, most of the tank battalions were broken up into company- or platoon-sized formations to support infantry operations. Typically, a tank company would be held in reserve behind the advancing infantry battalion and a platoon of tanks brought forward

Man O' War, an M4A1 tank of 763rd Tank Battalion, heading out from Jualita during the advance on Buruaen on October 24, 1944. A Filipino guide on top of the turret is providing directions to the tank commander.

when needed to overcome particularly determined Japanese strongpoints. When the terrain proved impossible, tank battalions were sometimes attached to divisional artillery to conduct indirect fire missions. For example, the 763rd Tank Battalion with the 96th Division was attached to the divisional artillery on November 20, 1944 and served in this role until the end of the campaign a month later.

The 3rd Platoon, Co. A, 44th Tank Battalion led by *Southern Cross*, during the fighting around Limon on Leyte on November 27, 1944.

By the end of November, the US X Corps had fought its way up to the Carigara plains and began pushing through the Japanese defenses around Limon toward the coastal plains of the Leyte peninsula. The two new Japanese light tank companies entered combat in early December around Limon and were gradually lost during fighting with the 24th Division along Breakneck Ridge, with the last three being scuttled in late December 1944. The advance by the XXIV Corps out the Buruaen area had been frustrated by the mountainous terrain to the west. As a result, XXIV Corps began moving units via the limited southward road network toward Baybay on the western coast to make an end run around the main Japanese defenses. The advance up the west coast picked up momentum in early December.

On November 23, the IJA decided to break the stalemate on the Buruaen front by staging Operation *Wa*, an airborne landing against the airstrips around Buruaen by the IJA 1st Parachute Training Regiment reinforced by local ground attacks. This began on the morning of December 6, but only the first phase of the airborne landings was completed before weather and mechanical problems grounded the transport aircraft. The airborne mission was suspended on December 7 due to the American amphibious landing at Ormoc described below. The XXIV Corps started a new counteroffensive on December 8 with tank support, causing the Imperial General Headquarters to order a general retreat by the 16th and 26th Divisions from the Buruaen front.

The X Corps' attacks toward northwestern Leyte were stymied by the continual arrival of Japanese reinforcements through the port of Ormoc on the western coast. In December 1944, the Sixth US Army decided to end this threat once and for all. The 7th Division moved northward from Baybay along the coastal highway, supported by amphibious tanks of the 778th Amphibious Tank Battalion acting as improvised gunboats from offshore. A task force based around the newly arrived 77th Division conducted an amphibious landing directly against Ormoc. Co. A, 778th Amphibious Tank Battalion took part in this landing, spearheading the attack on December 7. The amtanks became the first US forces into Ormoc on December 10. The Japanese response was to attempt to ship further reinforcements via Ormoc over the next several nights. This led to one of the most curious tank encounters of the Leyte campaign.

The Ormoc tank skirmish

At the time of the US landings at Ormoc, Japanese Convoy TA-9 was being organized near Manila to reinforce Leyte. It consisted of three transport

An LVT(A)4 amtank of the 776th Amphibian Tank Battalion supporting infantry units on Leyte in late 1944.

An M10 3in GMC of the Anti-tank Company, 307th Infantry on the shores of Ormoc Bay after the fighting with the Itoh Butai the previous night. In the background is the burning wreck of the Japanese tank landing ship *T.159* that had been pummeled by gunfire from the M10s, M8 75mm HMC, and LVT(A)4 amtanks on the night of December 11/12, 1944.

ships along with escorting destroyers and a few 2nd-class tank landing ships. These tank landing ships were assigned to deliver the Itoh Detachment. This SNLF detachment was led by Lt Cdr Tokuo Itoh and included Type 2 Ka-Mi amphibious tanks.

During the voyage to Ormoc, Convoy TA-9 was hit by about 40 US Marine F4U Corsair fighter-bombers off the Leyte coast. The two surviving tank landing ships, the *T.140* and *T.159*, carried nine Type 2 Ka-Mi tanks,

400 infantry, and a 20cm rocket artillery unit. They arrived in Ormoc Bay shortly before midnight on the night of December 11/12.

The Japanese naval commanders were confused about the location of the US forces. The convoy's first landing barge steered directly into Ormoc harbor and was blasted by 40mm Bofors guns and .50cal machine guns of the US 7th Antiaircraft Battalion. Around 2300hrs, the *T.159* approached the shore near Linao, east of Ormoc that was patrolled by the Cannon Company of the 307th Infantry, 77th Division. Lt Ted Bell's cannon platoon was equipped with two M8 75mm HMC assault guns and began firing at the *T.159*. They were quickly joined by a few M10 3in GMC tank destroyers of the regimental anti-tank company that were about 1,000yds from the *T.159*. Also in the vicinity were a few LVT(A)4 amtanks of Co. A, 776th Amphibian Tank Battalion, that joined the nighttime firefight. The Japanese landing ship returned ineffective fire with its deck-mounted antiaircraft guns. In response, the neighboring US infantry called in artillery fire to prevent any further Japanese troop landings. About 150 Japanese troops and two Type 2 Ka-Mi tanks had left the ship before the Japanese captain decided to withdraw to a safer anchorage. The *T.159* was barely 50yds from shore when it sank due to the many hits suffered in the engagement. It burned through the remainder of the night.

The *T.140* landed further to the west near Naguan and managed to disembark most of its troops and tanks before being spotted by the US troops. Discarded pontoons from the Type 2 Ka-Mi tanks were found on shore, so it is possible that at least a few of the tanks swam ashore. The *T.140* could barely be seen through the fire and smoke from the flaming wreck of *T.159*. At first light, *T.140* was taken under fire by the M10 3in GMCs of the anti-tank company. The *T.140* tried to withdraw by hugging the coast west of the landing site but was heavily damaged before finally escaping. Troops from the 307th Infantry overran the landing area after dawn. Eight of the nine Type 2 Ka-Mi tanks had disembarked; presumably one either sank or was trapped in the wreckage of *T.159*. Three had already

One of the Type 2 Ka-Mi amphibious tanks of the Itoh Butai that made it ashore on the night of December 11/12, 1944 in Ormoc Bay. It still has the engine deck snorkel in place but the front and rear pontoons have been dropped off after reaching shore.

been knocked out by American gunfire and four more were claimed by the infantry. One was captured intact. This was the last Japanese tank action of the Leyte campaign.

The end run to Ormoc doomed the Japanese defense of Leyte. A further blow came on December 15 when the Sixth US Army conducted an amphibious landing on Mindoro. The US capture of this island made it impossible for any further Japanese reinforcement of Leyte. On December 19, the US Army captured the headquarters of the Japanese 35th Army at Libongao, effectively ending any centralized control of the IJA units on Leyte. The Sixth US Army declared Leyte secure on December 26, although small-scale mop-up operations would continue deep in the mountains for several months.

A US Army study of the Luzon campaign concluded that:

> The use of tanks on Leyte left much to be desired. Many successful operations were conducted by tank units there, but many opportunities to use the tanks to telling advantage were overlooked or disregarded. Several reasons for this are apparent. In the first place, the terrain on the island was poor for tanks. In the training of the tank units, not enough emphasis was placed as to the nature of the ground over which they were to fight. In the second place, there was a serious lack of training between the tankers and the infantry resulting in a mutual misunderstanding of each other's capabilities and limitations.

Operation *Mike-1*: *Luzon*

Luzon is the main island in the Philippines and is the location of the capital city of Manila. The island contained extensive forested mountain areas similar to Leyte. However, there were several broad valleys far more suitable for tank operations than were present on Leyte.

The principal Japanese army force on Luzon was the 14th Area Army under Gen Tomoyuki Yamashita. By early 1945, it had been reduced to six infantry divisions, one tank division, and several garrison forces. Yamashita doubted that his forces could successfully resist an initial American amphibious landing. Instead of intending a decisive battle to defeat the US Army on Luzon, he planned a more limited objective of delaying the American conquest of Luzon and inflicting the maximum number of casualties. The most obvious operational objective on Luzon was Manila, but Yamashita

AMPHIBIOUS TANKS IN THE ORMOC BAY SKIRMISH

1. Type 2 Ka-Mi, 3rd Masaki Detachment, Itoh Butai, Ormoc Bay, December 1944. The initial production batches of Ka-Mi tanks were painted in the standard IJN dark gray that changed in late 1943 to the IJN's new Gaigen No. 21 dark green color as seen here. IJN tanks tended to carry the IJN ensign (as seen here). The Itoh Butai numbered their tanks by detachment with the HQ numbers being in the 1xx series, 1st Tsurusuki Detachment in the 3xx series, 2nd Murakami in the 5xx series, 3rd Masaki in the 6xx series, and 4th Furusato in the 2xx series. Besides the location on the turret side, the number was repeated on the rear of the hull preceded by the IJN anchor symbol, and on the rear of the snorkel trunk.

2. LVT(A)4, Co. A, 776th Amphibious Tank Battalion, Ormoc Bay, Leyte. Amtracs and amtanks were contracted by the US Navy and originally appeared in Ocean Gray 5-0, a blue-gray color. Complaints by army troops about the unsuitability of this color once the vehicle reached the shore led the army to issue Technical Bulletin ORD 102 on May 30, 1944 that authorized the repainting in standard lusterless olive drab as seen here. Markings on US Army amtanks tended to be very simple, in this case limited to a white star on the turret side.

An M4 of Co. A, 754th Tank Battalion with its deep-wading trunks still attached is seen passing in front of the Pangasinan Provincial Capitol building immediately inland from Lingayen beach during the amphibious landings on Luzon on January 9, 1945.

avoided a defense of the city, perhaps influenced by Douglas MacArthur's declaration of Manila as an open city in the 1941–42 campaign. Instead, he deployed the main elements of the 14th Area Army into three mountainous bastions for a prolonged campaign of attrition. Yamashita personally commanded the largest of these concentrations, the Shobu Group in the Cordillera Central and Sierra Madre mountains of northern Luzon.

A combat order issued by the IJA 2nd Armored Division on November 15, 1944, opened with the admonition: "This Philippines battle will end either in the annihilation of the American devils or in the complete destruction of our forces. The decisive day is drawing near ... Emphasis must be placed on anti-tank combat, especially against their heavy tanks. Our lack of armament is more than equaled by our divine ability and superior tactics."

Under early plans, most of the 2nd Armored Division was stationed on the Central Plains between the likely landing sites on the Lingayen Gulf and Manila. Its deployments changed several times in December prior to the American amphibious landings. Yamashita created the Kembu Group near Clark Field to threaten any American advance down the Manila plains. Although this was originally based on large elements of the 2nd Armored Division, many of these were stripped away, and the Kembu Group was left with a hodge-podge of improvised units.

During the first week of January 1945, Yamashita ordered the 2nd Armored Division to form a battlegroup to reinforce the 23rd Division that was holding the eastern shoulder of the Lingayen Gulf area. This was an especially vital assignment as not only did this sector adjoin the Lingayen Gulf, but it controlled the access routes into the mountainous bastion in northern Luzon.

When the American landings began on January 9, the remaining elements of the 2nd Armored were ordered from the Central Plains northwest to Tayug along the Agno River. The new assignment was to create a potential counterattack force to strike the left flank of any American attack down the Central Plains to Manila. At this stage, the division was broken up into three main chunks: the Takayama Group, formed from the 2nd Mobile Infantry Regiment, remained committed to the defense of Clark Field; the Shigemi Group, led by Maj Gen Isao Shigemi, commander of the 3rd Tank Brigade, was the vanguard of the division and moving toward Lingayen Gulf with the reinforced 7th Tank Regiment; and the majority of the division, including both the Ida Group (6th Tank Regiment) and Harada Group (10th Tank Regiment), was moving toward the Agno River line.

The Sixth US Army's Operation *Mike-1* plans were centered on the Lingayen Gulf on the west-central coast of Luzon, the same location where the Japanese Army had landed in 1941. The Lingayen Gulf offered excellent beaches with open terrain behind, providing a deep beachhead to build up forces for subsequent operations. It was at the northern end of the Central

One of the more obscure Japanese armored vehicles in the Philippines campaign was the Type 4 Ho-Ro 150mm assault gun. Three were deployed with Capt Sumi's independent gun company which was attached to the 2nd Armored Division's Takayama Detachment. They were knocked out during fighting with the US Army's 40th Infantry Division during the fighting near Fort Stotsenburg north of Manila in February 1945.

Plains corridor leading to Clark Field and Manila. Due to the potential threat of the 2nd Armored Division, the plans for the Luzon landings included a larger armor component than in previous campaigns in the Southwest Pacific. Each of the two corps taking part in the initial landings was assigned a single tank battalion for support, the 716th Tank Battalion with I Corps on the left flank, and the 754th Tank Battalion with the XIV Corps on the right flank. In addition, the 13th Armored Group landed two days later to act as a mobile reserve in the face of any Japanese tank thrust. The 13th Armored Group included the 44th and 775th Tank Battalions, the 632nd Tank Destroyer Battalion, and the 156th Engineer Combat Battalion.

The Shigemi Group was the first element of the IJA 2nd Armored Division to encounter US forces in the foothills east of the Lingayen beachhead. On January 10, Lt Gen Fukutaro Nishiyama, the 23rd Division commander, ordered the Shigemi Group to mass in the San Manuel area, and on January 12,

The 2nd Engineer Regiment of the 2nd Armored Division on Luzon had eight of these Type SS-Ki Tei Gata (Model D) armored engineer vehicles, based on components of the Type 89 medium tank. It was used primarily as a flamethrower tank armed with three flamethrowers. The four bins seen in the middle of the suspension were external tanks for the flame fuel. Other versions of this vehicle including the Type SS-Ki Bo Gata were also used by the regiment on Luzon. The regimental insignia is evident on the side.

The M7 105mm HMCs were used as assault guns by the infantry regiments in the Philippines. This is an M7 of the Cannon Company, 130th Infantry, 33rd Division moving into Naguilian, Luzon, on March 23, 1945.

he directed the group to move forward to destroy US tank units operating in the Cabaruan hills area. This was primarily the 716th Tank Battalion supporting the 43rd Division. On January 14, the 23rd Division ordered a simultaneous counterattack of the American beachhead in the pre-dawn hours of January 17 by four "suicide penetration units," three of these being from the infantry regiments, and the Takaki Detachment drawn from the Shigemi Group.

In the event, this major counterattack against the Lingayen beachhead degenerated into a series of disjointed and ineffective attacks. On January 17, a Japanese soldier described the fighting in his diary: "It's pitiful. The raid failed. The commanders of the Takaki Tank Detachment, 2nd Infantry Company, two tank platoon commanders, and one infantry platoon leader were all killed. Six tanks were destroyed and the two infantry companies lost half their troops."

On January 17, the 103rd Infantry, 25th Division took the lead and continued the attack into Binalonan where the remnants of the Takaki Detachment along with reinforcements from two tank companies of the 7th Tank Regiment had set up defensive positions. On January 18, the 161st Infantry, supported by Co. C, 716th Tank Battalion, cleared Binalonan. In the fight for the town, the 7th Tank Regiment lost nine tanks. The remnants of the forward detachments retreated to the main stronghold of the Shigemi Group in San Manuel in the pre-dawn darkness of January 19.

To the south, Co. A, 716th Tank Battalion assisted the 3/1st Infantry, 6th Infantry Division during an attack on Urdaneta on the morning of January 17. This town was garrisoned by other tank platoons of the 7th Tank Regiment with a company of infantry. The Japanese detachment in Urdaneta lost nine tanks and about 100 troops during this skirmish. In total, the fighting in the I Corps sector on January 16–17 cost the advance guards

ASSAULT GUNS IN THE PHILIPPINES

1. M8 75mm HMC, Cannon Company, 307th Infantry, 77th Division, Ormoc Bay, Leyte, December 1944. The M8 was finished in the usual lusterless olive drab. The markings are simple consisting of the vehicle name "Louise," and the US Army marking with the registration number below.

2. Type 1 Ho-Ni 1 self-propelled gun, 2nd Mobile Artillery Regiment, 2nd Armored Division, Luzon, December 1944. The self-propelled guns of this regiment were finished in the simplified 1942 scheme of parched grass, willow green, and mahogany brown. At least two variations of the insignia were seen on these, probably distinguishing batteries, one with a red disk and the other in white with a hollow rectangle within the center disk.

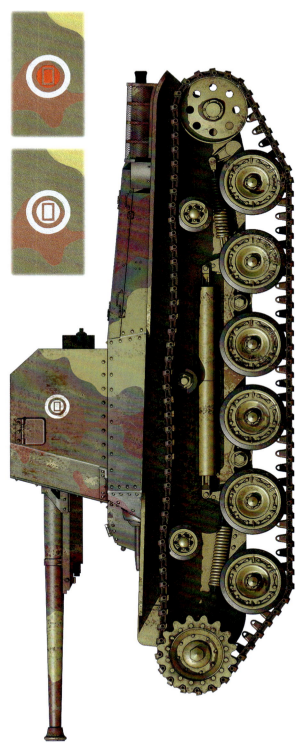

of the Shigemi Group a total of 19 Type 97 medium tanks and three Type 95 light tanks.

The San Manuel tank battle

By mid-January, Gen Yamashita was forced to reconsider his deployments when one of his infantry divisions failed to block access into the Cagayen Valley. Instead, he redirected the 2nd Armored Division from its defense sector north of San Nichols to move instead to Munoz and Lupao, shielding San Jose and the routes into the Cagayen Valley. The Shigemi Group was ordered to remain behind and to hold the town of San Manuel to cover the rest of the 2nd Armored Division while they redeployed in front of San Jose. On January 20, Gen Shigemi issued orders to his forces in San Manuel: "The group will defend its present position to the death. The enemy must be annihilated and we will hold San Manuel at all costs."

The tactics for the defense of San Manuel were to use the tanks as semi-mobile pillboxes, operating from hull-down entrenchments. The town was ringed with tank revetments, and inner layers of revetments were dug inside the town to allow the tanks to cover major roads, streets, and intersections. The tank revetments had an accompanying set of rifle pits and machine gun emplacements for infantry defense. The defenses took advantage of the extensive vegetation at the edges of the town. A total of about 75 tank revetments were constructed, more than enough for the depleted 7th Tank Regiment which by this stage had only about 50 tanks. Many of the troops in the "spider hole" defenses near the tanks were from divisional service units not trained as infantry. The decision to entrench the division's tanks was controversial, and the source of considerable criticism after the fighting.

The 7th Tank Regiment deployed about half of its tanks in shallow revetments throughout San Manuel. This Type 97-kai had left the protection of its revetment, which is seen in the foreground.

The reduction of San Manuel was assigned to the 161st Regimental Combat Team (RCT) consisting of two of the 161st Infantry's three battalions, supported by Co. C and Co. D, 716th Tank Battalion, and a 4.2in mortar battalion. The 161st RCT received fire support from several field artillery battalions for much of the operation. First blood was drawn on January 19 when light tanks of Co. D, 716th Tank Battalion, came under an intense volley of tank fire while scouting near the western outskirts of San Manuel. Two M5A1 light tanks were lost. The 161st RCT began its attack on January 24 with the main blow from the 2/161st Infantry against the northern section of the town, and a secondary blow against the southwest corner of the town by the 1/161st Infantry supported by Co. C, 716th Tank Battalion.

The M4A3 tanks of Co. C reached to within 300yds of the southwestern corner of the town before the preparatory US artillery barrage lifted. Japanese fire discipline was strict, and the M4A3 tanks were not engaged until they were at

point-blank range of about 150yds. At this point, the tanks were suddenly raked by tank gun and machine gun fire. Several tanks were hit and at least one became jammed in an irrigation canal.

The 161st RCT's later report complained that tanks were not very useful in attacks such as these across open ground. The 161st Infantry was not experienced in the use of tanks and, like many veteran units, it tended to disparage Japanese anti-tank firepower. There was an unstated expectation that M4A3 medium tanks were essentially invulnerable to Japanese AT guns. This was certainly the case with the old 37mm gun, but not with the new Japanese 47mm gun. Instead of remaining at stand-off range to provide fire support while the infantry advanced to the edge of the town, the Shermans were expected to charge into the town.

After several failed attacks, reinforcements arrived in the afternoon including four M7 105mm HMCs from the regimental Cannon Company, and six 37mm AT guns from the regimental anti-tank company. A renewed attack at 1700hrs secured a foothold after five Type 97-kai tanks defending this sector were engaged and knocked out by gunfire.

On January 25, the 2/161st Infantry began a systematic block-by-block assault through the northern section of San Manuel. The new tactic was to assign an infantry scout to each tank or self-propelled howitzer. The scout would escort the vehicle commander forward and show him the intended target. The vehicle commander could then direct his tank or self-propelled howitzer forward to an advantageous position and destroy the emplaced Japanese tank or gun revetment.

This is a Type 97-kai Shinhoto Chi-Ha of the 3rd Company, 7th Tank Regiment knocked out during the Binalonan fighting.

Lt Kunio Nagabuchi's 1st Tank Company, 7th Tank Regiment was equipped with the Type 95 light tank and one of these tanks is seen destroyed in front of a house in San Manuel after the fighting.

The M7 105mm HMC was generally preferred for this task, in spite of the open crew compartment. The much more powerful high-explosive round of the 105mm howitzer was able to strip away camouflage on the Japanese revetments and was more than adequate to demolish the lightly armored Japanese tanks. By January 27, most of the north half of the town had been captured. A two-battalion attack with tank and M7 105mm HMC support began after another heavy artillery preparation.

With the defenses crumbling, Shigemi ordered a final counterattack shortly after midnight. A US report described the attack:

> About 0100 28 January the Japs, after a great deal of preliminary maneuvering, launched an attack with thirteen tanks. The point was well selected: a salient made by the left company of the right flank battalion [1/161st Infantry]. Normal barrages of artillery and mortar were called in but did not quiet the Japs. The tanks assaulted in waves of three, each tank followed closely by foot troops. The tank assault position was about 100–150 yards from our foremost elements. Riflemen in pits opposed them with rifle AT grenades, bazookas and caliber .50 machine guns. Two 37mm guns had the tanks within range. The first tank was hit but overran the forward position, spraying blindly with machine guns and firing 47mm point-blank. Two AT guns set about 30 to 40 yards in the rear of the front elements fired on the waves in turn. Ten of the tanks were halted, the leading one just 50 yards inside our front. All had been hit several times. Hits and penetrations were made with AT shells, AT grenades, bazookas and caliber .50 machine guns. Three tanks left the assault position and withdrew eastward out of town without attacking.

In the wake of the failed attack, Gen Shigemi committed *hara-kiri* (ritual suicide). Surviving Japanese troops numbering about 400 men and seven tanks fled out through the southeastern side of the town toward San

Old Sarge, an M7 105mm HMC of the Cannon Company of the 161st Infantry, 25th Division credited with the destruction of 12 Japanese tanks and four artillery pieces during the fighting with the Shigemi Group of the IJA 2nd Armored Division at San Manuel in February 1945. One crewman was wounded when the vehicle was hit during the fighting which accounts for the Purple Heart decoration painted in front of the kill markings.

Nichols. San Manuel was declared secure at 1330hrs on January 29 after six days of fighting. The Shigemi Detachment lost 41 Type 97 medium tanks and four Type 95 light tanks in the fighting, while the 716th Tank Battalion lost two M5A1 light tanks and five M4A3 medium tanks.

The tank battle at Munoz

After the reduction of San Manuel, the I Corps ordered the 6th and 25th Divisions to conduct a pincer attack against the main Japanese stronghold at San Jose. This led to two simultaneous tank battles against the 2nd Armored Division in the first week of February, with the 6th Division confronting the Ida Group in Munoz and the 25th Division attacking the Harada Group at Lupao.

The Ida Group in Munoz, commanded by Col Kumpai Ida, the commanding officer of the 6th Tank Regiment, was similar in size to the Shigemi Group with a strength of 48 Type 97 medium tanks, four Type 95 light tanks, four armored cars, and 1,800 troops; the group was reinforced with 16 47mm AT guns and a battery of four 105mm field guns. The Ida Group followed the practice of constructing numerous tank revetments along the edge of the town with additional strongpoints inside the town itself.

The attack on Munoz was undertaken by the 20th RCT, including the 20th Infantry, 6th Infantry Division, supported by Co. C, 44th Tank Battalion and a company of 4.2in mortars. The town had been heavily bombarded by both artillery and air strikes starting on January 28 and hardly any buildings were left intact. A company-sized attack on Munoz on January 31 secured a small foothold and was followed by a battalion-sized attack. On February 1, two battalions attacked the town from the southwest. The fighting on February 2 ended in stalemate although an attempted counterattack by the Ida Group was repulsed with heavy Japanese casualties. The 6th Division commander realized that the size of the Ida Group had been substantially underestimated. The renewed attacks on February 3 included all three battalions of the 20th RCT along with tank support, but the fighting turned into a stubborn and frustrating block-by-block siege.

While the 20th RCT was engaged with the Ida Group at Munoz, the 25th Division on its left attacked the scattered 2nd Armored Division garrisons on the approaches to Lupao. The Omura Detachment in Gonzales included a company of the 6th Tank Regiment and two motorized artillery companies. At 1800hrs on the night of January 29, the Omura Detachment was ordered to retire from Gonzales to San Jose along Highway 8. In the dark, the column stumbled into the defensive perimeter of the 27th Infantry,

On the night of January 29–30, the Omura Detachment attempted to withdraw from Gonzales to San Jose along the Pemienta–Umingan section of Highway 8. The column stumbled into American roadblocks including tanks of Co. C, 716th Tank Battalion and was wiped out. This is one of eight Type 97-kai Shinhoto Chi-Ha's of Capt Shoji Arao's 2nd Company, 6th Tank Regiment destroyed in the fighting. Spare tracks were attached to the turret front for additional protection, to no avail.

E   **TANK BATTLE ON THE APPROACHES TO THE SAN JOSE MOUNTAIN REDOUBT, JANUARY 1945**

Here, an M4A3 tank named *Classy Peg* of Co. C, 716th Tank Battalion, passes a smoldering Type 97-kai Shinhoto Chi-Ha of the Takaki Detachment of the 4th Company, 7th Tank Regiment which had been knocked out during the fighting around Binalonan on January 17, 1945.

An M18 76mm GMC of Co. B, 637th Tank Destroyer Battalion, supporting the 129th Infantry, 37th Division during the fighting near Baguio, Luzon on April 24, 1945. Baguio was the summer capital of the Philippines and the 129th Infantry was the first regiment into the city that day.

25th Division around Pemienta, supported by Co. C, 716th Tank Battalion. A six-hour firefight ensued that lasted until dawn on January 30. In the process, the Omura Detachment was largely destroyed including eight Type 97-kai tanks.

The 27th Infantry faced far stiffer resistance at Umingan, facing an entrenched infantry regiment with at least eight 47mm AT guns. When it failed to secure Umingan on February 1, the 25th Division ordered the neighboring 35th Infantry to bypass the town and proceed toward Lupao. This was defended by the Harada Group in two clusters, first in Lupao and then in San Isidro further to the southeast. The Harada Group, commanded by Lt Col Kazuo Harada, commander of the 10th Tank Regiment, included four tank companies and an anti-tank gun company.

The initial attacks on Lupao on February 2–3 by the 35th Infantry were frustrated by concentrated fire from the dug-in Japanese tanks. By this stage, the 6th and 25th Division commanders had finally realized that Lupao and Munoz were as heavily fortified as San Manuel. Unwilling to take heavy casualties to reduce these bastions, both divisions decided to continue limited sieges to keep the Japanese forces in place, while other regiments bypassed them to secure the main objective at San Jose.

While both divisions were expecting a major fight for San Jose on February 4, it turned out to be an anticlimax. The 1st Infantry, 6th Division marched into the city virtually unopposed on the morning of February 4 against a tiny Japanese rearguard and secured the city by 1330hrs with very light casualties.

Brassiereless Baby, an M4 of Co. B, 775th Tank Battalion advances up a steep hill on the outskirts of Baguio, Luzon on April 27, 1945 during the final efforts to liberate the city.

The Japanese 2nd Armored Division were unaware that Gen Yamashita's 14th Area Army Headquarters had issued instructions on February 4 for all units to withdraw since the main mission of the 2nd Armored Division, to delay the American offensive, had already been accomplished. The IJA 2nd Armored Division Headquarters did not receive the withdrawal order until February 6.

By this time, the Ida Group in Munoz had been battered by several days of artillery bombardment. Col Ida had been killed and 35 tanks had been knocked out. The Ida Group attempted a breakout on the night of February 6–7, not realizing that the escape route was firmly in American hands. The Japanese column first ran into roadblocks established by the 63rd Infantry, but then was brought under point-blank fire by 105mm and 155mm howitzers of the 53rd and 80th Field Artillery Battalions and an M4 tank company of the 44th Tank Battalion. The escaping column was wiped out. Japanese casualties during the battle of Munoz were 52 tanks and 1,527 troops.

The Harada Group in Lupao and San Isidro sabotaged most surviving vehicles and heavy equipment and tried to slip away into the mountains in the darkness. In Lupao, one tank detachment of 10–11 tanks raced out of the town after dark. About half were destroyed, while five escaped into the hills. Lupao was cleared on February 8. By the end of the first week of February, the Japanese 2nd Armored Division in northern Luzon had lost about 180 tanks as well as most of its artillery equipment and about 2,000 troops. By the first week of March after the northern Luzon area had been scoured, the tally rose to 197 Chi-Ha and 19 Ha-Go tanks.

Although the Japanese 2nd Armored Division had lost nearly all of its tanks, tank crews, motorized infantry units, and other heavy equipment, it continued to fight through to the end of the Philippines campaign. The 14th Area Army used the division's headquarters and service elements to reconstitute it as an improvised infantry division.

The battle for Manila

During January–February 1945, while I Corps confronted the 2nd Armored Division in the northeast of Luzon, XIV Corps began its advance southward

The elements of the 2nd Armored Division left behind to defend Clark Field included an independent tank company from the 6th Tank Regiment, called the Iwashita Detachment after its commander. The company's attempts to counterattack on January 27–29 led to severe losses as is seen here when two of the company's tanks were destroyed on January 27.

Battle Basic, the M4 tank with Capt Jesse L. Walters and his crew after the battle of Manila. Walters was the commander of Co. B, 44th Tank Battalion and this tank was the first to break into the Santo Tomas University to rescue interned civilian prisoners on February 3, 1945.

to Manila. Although Gen Yamashita had not planned a major defense of the Central Plains leading to Manila, there was a belated effort to defend the most important military objectives in the area, Clark Field and Fort Stotsenburg. Maj Gen Rikichi Tsukada was placed in charge of the Kembu Group which was based on the 2nd Mobile Infantry Regiment of the 2nd Armored Division along with the 2nd Glider Infantry Regiment. There were a further 20,000 miscellaneous army and navy personnel in the area from airfield battalions, antiaircraft units and rear service forces. The only significant tank unit in the area was Lt Matsumoto's 8th Ind. Tank Company equipped with Type 89 tanks, and the Iwashita Ind. Tank Company from the 6th Tank Regiment with eight Type 97-kai tanks.

The XIV Corps began its assault on Clark Field on January 28 consisting primarily of the 37th and 40th Divisions. Based on the Leyte lessons, the 754th Tank Battalion had practiced tank–infantry cooperation prior to the campaign. The battalion later attributed its superior performance during the campaign to this vital cross-training.

The Yanagimoto Detachment of the Kembu Group launched a counterattack on the afternoon of January 29 during which the Iwashita Tank Company was destroyed; four of the Japanese tanks credited to the 637th Tank Destroyer Battalion. As the 37th Division gradually won control of Clark Field, Yamashita ordered many of the remaining elements of the Kembu Group into the Zambales mountains to the west to prolong the struggle. On January 29, the XI Corps was landed on the west coast at San Antonio including the 38th Division to prevent the Kembu Group from withdrawing to the Bataan peninsula. On January 31, the US 188th Glider Infantry Regiment spearheaded an amphibious assault of the 11th Airborne Division near Nasugbu on the southern approaches to Manila, enveloping the capital from all sides.

SHINHOTO CHI-HA TANKS OF THE 2ND ARMORED DIVISION ON LUZON 1945

1. Type 97-kai, Iwashita Detachment, 2nd Armored Division, Clark Field, January 1945. This Shinhoto Chi-Ha is in the standard 1942 finish of overall parched grass with bands of willow green and mahogany brown. The three tank regiments of the 2nd Armored Division used insignia derived from the *Sakura* (cherry blossom) but with a square in the center (6th Tank Regiment), circle (7th Tank Regiment), and X (10th Tank Regiment) as seen in the inset drawing. The other insignia on the hull side is unexplained; it is similar to the "folded fan" insignia of the 2nd Mobile Infantry Regiment to which the detachment was attached. The Japanese character "I" in Katakana seen on the turret presumably refers to the detachment commander, Capt Iwashita.

2. Type 97-kai, 2nd Armored Division, 3rd Company, 7th Tank Regiment, 2nd Armored Division, Luzon, Philippines, January 1945. This Shinhoto Chi-Ha is in the simplified 1942 finish of overall parched grass with bands of willow green and mahogany brown. The 7th Tank Regiment were marked with the usual Japanese cherry blossom insignia with a circle inside. The marking in front of it is the traditional *"Tomoe"* design, derived from the family crest of Oishi Kuranosuke, leader of the legendary 47 Ronin warriors of 1702. On the side of the gun cover is an Ai-koku presentation marking consisting of two stylized circular characters above, and the symbols for *Dai Nippon* (Greater Japan) below.

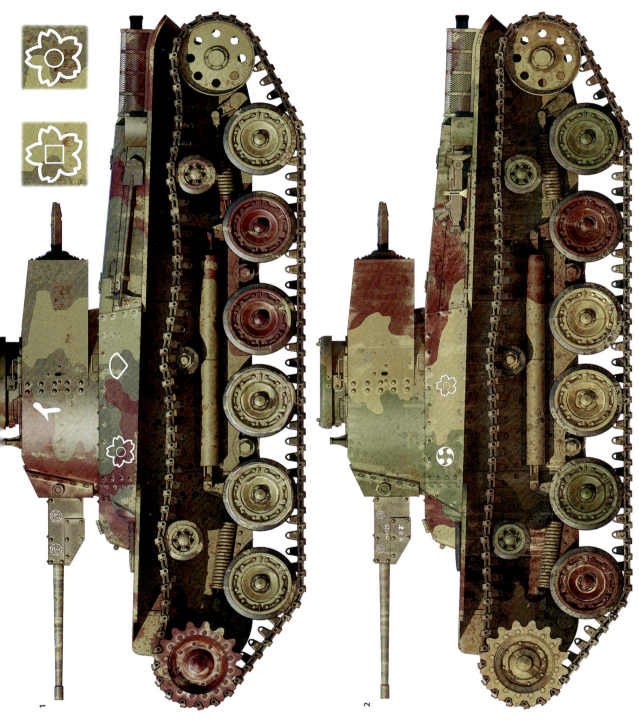

The first mission of the "flying column" of the 44th Tank Battalion in Manila on February 3 was the liberation of civilian prisoners who had been interned by the Japanese at the Santo Tomas University since 1942. Here, the freed civilians visit the crew of "Broadway Terror," an M4 of Co. B, 44th Tank Battalion.

Yamashita had planned for little more than a token defense of Manila itself, and withdrew his main force, the Shimbu Group, into the mountains east of the city. Rear Adm Sanji Iwabuchi, commander of the Manila Naval Defense Force (MNDF), had very different ideas. The Manila garrison included 13,000 miscellaneous naval personnel assigned to provisional infantry battalions as well as about 4,000 army troops. Although poorly trained for ground combat, the improvised naval units were amply equipped with naval guns, automatic cannon, and heavy machine guns stripped from sunken ships and wrecked aircraft in the area. Yamashita's limited objectives for the MNDF had been the destruction of bridges to impede the American advance and the evacuation of supplies, after which the Manila garrison was to withdraw into the mountains to the east to reinforce the Shimbu Group's defensive efforts. The IJN Southwest Area Fleet Headquarters gave Iwabuchi far broader goals to destroy all naval installations and supplies in Manila and neighboring Cavite, a scheme that presumed a prolonged defense of Manila.

The American advance on Manila was spearheaded by a "flying column" of the 44th Tank Battalion and the 8th Cavalry Regiment of the 1st Cavalry Division. It reached the outskirts of Manila in the first days of February. Their immediate mission on February 3 was to liberate the 3,500 civilian internees from the 1941–42 campaign at Santo Tomas University. The flying column was followed by the 37th Division and 1st Cavalry Division from the north and the 11th Airborne Division from the south. During the first week of

Although the color quality of this photo has deteriorated, it provides a rare glimpse of one of the few Japanese tanks used by the MNDF, an M3 light tank captured in the 1942 campaign. It was photographed near Hotel Manila and it may have been the tank knocked out on Padre Faura Street, a few blocks from the hotel. It is missing its 37mm gun.

February, the XIV Corps units gradually cleared the suburbs of Manila north of the Pasig River. The subsequent objective was the capture of key city infrastructure, especially water supplies and key elements of the electrical network.

On the afternoon of February 7, the 37th Division shuttled over the Pasig River using amtracs of the 672nd Amphibian Tractor Battalion; the 1st Cavalry Division followed on February 10. A Special Security Force was created from the 637th Tank Destroyer Battalion, the 37th Cavalry Reconnaissance Troop, and Co. A, 754th Tank Battalion to complete the mop-up of Japanese forces north of the Pasig River. In the south, the 11th Airborne Division captured Nichols Field. The commander of the Shimbu Group, Lt Gen Shizuo Yokoyama, ordered Iwabuchi to withdraw the MNDF into the mountains east of the city; Iwabuchi ignored these instructions. Yokoyama was badly informed about the size of the attacking American force. Believing it to be only a regiment in strength, he ordered a counterattack by elements of the Shimbu Group east of the city on the night of February 16–17. This and subsequent attacks were handily repulsed.

Miette, an M4A1 tank of Co. A, 754th Tank Battalion pushed through the heavily damaged gate of Fort Santiago during the fighting for the walled city of Intramuros in Manila on February 26, 1945.

Tokyo or Bust, an M4 of the HQ Company's tank section providing fire support for the 1st Cavalry Division in the hills east of Manila on March 10, 1945.

The fighting for Manila began in earnest during the second week of February. The governmental district of the city was composed of modern earthquake-proof buildings constructed from steel-reinforced concrete. These were ideally suited for defensive purposes as was the old Spanish walled city of Intramuros. Two tank and one tank destroyer battalion took part in the urban battle for Manila. Their firepower proved invaluable in attacking Japanese strongholds. Nevertheless, the stout concrete buildings and the huge walls of Intramuros were resistant to 75mm guns. The assault gun platoon of the 716th Tank Battalion was dispatched to Manila since the 105mm howitzer of the M4 assault guns was more effective in urban fighting than the usual 75mm tank guns. The 76mm guns of the M18 76mm GMC of the 837th Tank Destroyer Battalion were found to be more effective due to their high velocity. M7 105mm HMC self-propelled howitzers of the infantry cannon companies were also widely used for attacking reinforced structures. The main threats to tanks in Manila were large-caliber guns, often taken from ships, as well as mines. Many of the mines were improvised from aircraft bombs and naval mines, and so were unusually large and destructive.

Aside from the usual destructiveness of urban warfare, the mission of the MNDF to demolish military infrastructure degenerated into wanton devastation of civilian infrastructure as well.

A view from the doorway of St Scholastica Church on Taft Avenue in Manila as *The Crusader*, an M4 tank of the 44th Tank Battalion, crunches past a street-car during the street fighting in Manila on February 16, 1945. In the seven days of fighting in this sector, Co. B expended 3,800 rounds of 75mm tank gun ammunition and 185,000 rounds of machine gun ammunition.

The MNDF was composed of an assortment of sailors and rear area troops with no tactical training and little leadership. The US Army history of the campaign later recalled that "Japanese command disintegrated … viciousness became uncontrolled and uncontrollable; horror mounted upon horror. The men of the 37th Infantry Division and the 1st Cavalry Division witnessed the rape, sack, pillage, and destruction of a large part of Manila." Numerous Filipino civilians were killed in the street fighting, but many more were deliberately massacred by vengeful Japanese troops leading to the deaths of more than 100,000 civilians in the battle.

The attack on the walled city of Intramuros began on February 23. Intramuros was the original fort built by the Spanish Conquistadores in the Manila Bay area in 1571. Heavy artillery was brought into the city to breach the wall with point-blank fire, assisted by the 637th Tank Destroyer Battalion. The fighting inside the city continued until March 3, 1945. US casualties were over 1,000 dead and 5,500 wounded; few of the Japanese garrison of 16,000 survived. There was little Japanese armor in Manila.

G

SHERMAN TANKS ON LUZON 1945

1. M4 Composite, Co. A, 775th Tank Battalion, Lingayen Gulf, January 1945. The 775th Tank Battalion used different markings styles for each company. Co. A as seen here used a pair of dice. The tank name, *Adulteress Model*, used the company letter at the beginning of the name in usual US Army fashion. The crew has added additional markings such as *Pat's Palace* on a plaque on the spare track on the turret, and a slogan on the gun barrel *"Shoot You're Faded."* Co. B used a shamrock and "B" names such as *Battle Baby*, *Battl'n Virgin*, etc. Co. C used cartoons and "C" names such as *Corsair* and *Cover Girl*. The battalion assault guns used a white circle with two cartoon boxing gloves.

2. M4A1, Co. A, 754th Tank Battalion, Fort Santiago, Manila, February 1945. The 754th Tank Battalion used geometric shapes for each company including a diamond for the HQ Company, a square for Co. A, a triangle for Co. B, a Circle for Co. C, and a large "D" for Co. D. The platoon was identified by a vertical stripe, one for 1st Platoon, etc. Tank names did not always follow the company letter practice as is evident here. *Miette* is the tank that broke into Fort Santiago. This tank lacks the usual large air identification star and the hull star has been overpainted.

1

2

An old M3 light tank, captured in 1942, was knocked out on Padre Faura Street on February 16 and an armored car was hit on Dewey Boulevard the same day.

The first month's fighting from roughly February 6 to March 5, 1945 was the most intense period of combat for the Sixth US Army on Luzon. The city of Manila had been captured, the Central Luzon Plains had been cleared of organized resistance, the IJA 2nd Armored Division had been gutted, and key military strongholds such as Bataan, Corregidor, and Cavite had been captured. Of the roughly 260,000 Japanese troops, about 110,000 remained active in northern Luzon while a further 60,000 were scattered elsewhere on the island. By this stage, most Japanese tanks had been lost, though there were still some scattered remnants of the 2nd Armored Division in the northern mountains.

The fighting over the next several months was directed against the remaining Japanese units scattered over Luzon, especially in the northern mountains. Tanks continued in their usual role of providing fire support for the infantry divisions.

Operation *Victor*: the final campaigns in the Philippines

The next major objective in the Philippines after Luzon was the Southern Visayas Islands that included Panay, Negros, Cebu, and Bohol. These were the assignments of the Eighth US Army. Operation *Victor-1* was based on the 40th Division, supported by two companies of the 716th Tank Battalion. Amphibious landings on Panay began on March 18. The Japanese defenses on the island had been stripped to support the defense of Leyte and consisted mainly of the 170th Ind. Infantry Battalion. Japanese resistance was largely overcome by March 21. The Panay operation was followed on March 29 by landings on the Negros Occidental Island, with two companies of the 716th Tank Battalion again providing the tank support. The principal Japanese force in the Negros was the 77th Infantry Brigade along with improvised units formed from airfield personnel and other service troops.

Black Beauty, an M4A3 of Co. B, 716th Tank Battalion is seen here with its full water-proofing and deep-wading kit in place on March 26, 1945 after having landed at Talisay, east of Cebu City during Operation *Victor-2* on Cebu. The company's wolf's-head insignia is visible on the turret while Co. C usually painted it on the hull side.

An M5A1 of Co. D, 716th Tank Battalion leads a column from the 40th Division on the outskirts of Bacolod shortly after the landings on Negros Island on March 29, 1945.

Japanese troops withdrew into a mountain redoubt east of Bacolod in early April that was largely overcome by the end of the month. On June 4, the US Army turned the final clean-up operation over to the re-born Philippine Army. The 716th Tank Battalion proved to be a valuable contribution to Operation *Victor-1* since, by this stage, the tactics of tank–infantry cooperation had become more established than in the earlier campaigns.

The objective of Operation *Victor-2* was the island of Cebu with landings beginning on March 26. The principal US Army formation was the Americal Division, supported by Co. B, 716th Tank Battalion. As elsewhere in the Visayas, the IJA forces were heavily depleted by earlier transfers to Leyte and the only significant unit was the 173rd Ind. Infantry Battalion. The navy's 33rd Special Base Force, based in Cebu City, was hastily organized for ground defense with total Japanese strength on the island totaling 14,500 troops at the time of the landings. The landing beaches were heavily mined and Japanese defenses on Cebu proved to be more determined than elsewhere in the Visayas. Fighting around Cebu City continued until April 20, and mop-up operations lingered well into early June. The tanks were generally doled out to the infantry in small groups and were most effective in the early phase of the fighting before the actions in the neighboring mountains limited the tanks' mobility.

Operation *Victor-4* was directed against the Zamboanga peninsula on the western side of Mindanao, and the Sulu archipelago. The mission was assigned to the 41st Division, supported by Co. A, 716th Tank Battalion. This was the only phase of the larger Mindanao campaign where tanks took part. The landings began on March 10 and the fighting lasted over a month. On April 7, Co. A, 716th Tank Battalion was transferred to the 163rd RCT for landings on nearby Jolo. The tanks supported the infantry battalions through the middle of April at which time the company was withdrawn for prolonged maintenance due to its extensive use the previous month. Mop-up operations continued in the Philippines through June 1945.

ANALYSIS

The most controversial aspect of the Philippines campaign from the Japanese perspective was Yamashita's decision to disperse the 2nd Armored Division into several village strongholds. Other Japanese officers felt this was a waste of an elite unit that should have been used in a heroic, decisive battle on the Central Plains of Luzon to thwart the American advance on Manila. Yamashita was skeptical about the division's ability to conduct such a mobile operation due to the obsolescence of the Japanese tanks, the overwhelming firepower available to American ground forces, and the vulnerability of the division to American air attack if used in open terrain. Regardless of the proper tactics, the Philippines campaign was evidence of how badly the Japanese armored force had declined in technology and tactics since 1941–42.

There were far more modest expectations for the US Army's tank battalions largely due to the limitations imposed by terrain and weather. Nevertheless, most officers felt that the tank battalions provided a valuable contribution to what was primarily an infantry battle. Lt Col Eric Ramee, an infantry battalion commander with the 24th Division, remarked in a post-war report that: "The simple presence of tanks is extremely valuable psychologically. Partly it's to see something on your side that is large and powerful moving toward the enemy. Even more, it's the idea that you afoot are not moving forward personally against an unseen enemy but you are moving forward with the welcome responsibility of protecting someone else – the tanks."

Iron Horse, an M4A3 of Co. A, 716th Tank Battalion in support of riflemen of the 41st Division on the Zamboanga peninsula on Mindanao in March 1945 during Operation *Victor-4*.

Conversely, the tank was an especially potent threat to the Japanese defenders as recalled in a study of the use of tanks on Leyte:

Even in close and jungled terrain, no other weapon causes so much consternation to the [Japanese] as the appearance or possible threat of armor. It creates, in the mind of the enemy commander, a feeling of doubt as to the adequacy of his preparations and defenses. It makes every man fearful that they are coming his way. In the worst of circumstance, the employment of armor contributes this psychological effect and is therefore worthwhile.

US tanks played a far more significant role in the Luzon campaign than on Leyte, both in the numbers of tanks used and the duration of the combat. This is very evident when comparing ammunition expenditure with the US Army using about six times more 75mm tank gun ammunition on Luzon than Leyte.

US tank and AFV ammunition expenditure on Leyte

Type	Oct 20–31	Nov 1–15	Nov 16–30	Dec 1–15	Dec 16–25	Total
75mm	2,838	3,034	1,077	4,991	1,762	**13,702**
3in	0	3,763	0	1,395	254	**5,412**
Total	**2,838**	**6,797**	**1,077**	**6,386**	**2,016**	**19,114**

US AFV strength/ammunition expenditure on Luzon 1945

	Jan 9–Feb 27	Feb 28–Mar 30	Mar 31–Apr 30	May 1–31	Jun 1–30	Total
Avg. strength						
M4 tanks	n/a	229	204	183	175	-
M18 TD	n/a	36	36	36	36	-
Ammunition use						
75mm	28,116	7,717	22,108	14,763	8,820	**81,524**
76mm	8,388	1,304	3,306	785	1,613	**15,396**
Total	**36,504**	**9,021**	**25,414**	**15,548**	**10,433**	**96,920**

An M3 light tank was knocked out by air attack in the June 1945 fighting near Tuguegarao in northern Luzon. A detachment of three of these tanks, captured from the US Army in 1942, was supporting the 103rd Division in this sector at the time.

The 5th Tank Company, 10th Tank Regiment escaped into the hills after the fighting around Lupao. In May 1945, Yamashita ordered the 2nd Armored Division to withdraw from the Villa Verde trail and most of the remaining tanks established defenses near Aritao. This Type 97-kai was knocked out during the fighting in early June by the 37th Division which was supported by the 775th Tank Battalion.

The tanks' primary role of infantry fire support was reflected in its ammunition usage on Luzon with 82.3 percent high explosive, 8.1 percent smoke, 2.9 percent cannister, and only 6.7 percent armor-piercing. Furthermore, much of the armor-piercing ammunition was used against hard targets such as concrete buildings rather than enemy tanks.

The principal cause of US tank losses in the Philippines was mines as is shown in the accompanying table. In many cases these were emplaced aircraft bombs and so were unusually destructive. Although detailed statistics are lacking, probably more Sherman tanks were knocked out by Japanese 47mm towed AT guns than by Japanese tank fire, since they were much more common and much more widespread on the islands. Although the 47mm gun could not penetrate the Sherman's frontal armor, it could penetrate the side armor at the short ranges typical in the Philippines fighting.

Source of US Army tank casualties in the Philippines

Percent	Mines	Gunfire	Other weapons	Non-enemy*
Philippines	42.6	29.4	18.4	9.6
Pacific (average)	27.7	33.8	18.8	19.7

Accidents, etc.

There are no comprehensive statistics for US tank strength or losses in the Philippines campaign since the corps and army headquarters lacked an armor section. Some battalion reports give a more detailed picture of combat losses. For example, on Leyte the 763rd Tank Battalion had two light tanks and 58 medium tanks disabled of which 30 were caused by mines and ten by satchel charges. The battalion suffered the total loss of 30 tanks consisting of one M5A1 light tank and 29 Shermans with 13 lost to mines, eight to AT guns, and one to satchel charges. On Luzon, the 754th Tank Battalion had 17 Sherman tanks damaged and five completely lost during the Luzon campaign.

FURTHER READING

This book was based primarily on primary sources including tank battalion after-action reports, US Army G-2 reports on Japanese units, and a variety of post-war US Army studies. The photos here are all from official US sources, mainly the US Army Signal Corps collections.

Unpublished studies and reports
Anon., *Japanese Defense of Cities as Exemplified by the Battle for Manila*, S-2, US Army XIV Corps, 1945

Anon., *Operation Report: XXIV Corps on Leyte*, US Army XXIV Corps, 1945

Anon., *Report of the Commanding General Eighth US Army on the Leyte–Samar Operation*, Eighth US Army, 1945

Anon., *Report of the Luzon Campaign 9 January 1945–30 June 1945*, Sixth US Army, 1945

Barrow, Capt Thomas, *Breakthrough to Manila*, US Army Armored School, Fort Knox, 1948

Garay, Maj Stephen, *The Breach of Intramuros*, US Army Armored School, Fort Knox, 1948

Harrison, Lt Col Walter, *The Suicide Stand at San Manuel*, Sixth US Army, 1945

Hunt, Maj Milton, *Use of Armor on Luzon*, US Army Armored School, Fort Knox, 1948

Jensen, Capt Denmark, *The Operations of the Cannon Company, 17th Infantry on Leyte October 1944*, Infantry School, Fort Benning, 1949

Johnson, Capt Charles, *Operation of the Cannon Company, 32nd Infantry Regiment on Leyte, P.I. October 1944*, Infantry School, Fort Benning, 1949

McElhenney, Lt Col, et al., *Armor on Luzon*, US Army Armored School, Fort Knox, 1950

Sipes, Lt Col Kenneth, et al., *Armor in Island Warfare*, US Army Armored School, Fort Knox, 1950

Tomochika, Maj Gen Yoshiharu, *The True Facts of the Leyte Operation*, Historical Service, Eighth US Army, 1945

Books
Anon., *Japanese Operations in the Southwest Pacific Area: Volume II, Part II of the Reports of General MacArthur*, US Army, Washington DC, 1966

Cannon, Hamlin, *Leyte: The Return to the Philippines*, US Army Center of Military History, Washington DC, 1954

Dick, Robert, *Cutthroats: The Adventures of a Sherman Tank Driver in the Pacific*, Presidio, Novato, 2006

Salecker, Gene, *Rolling Thunder against the Rising Sun: The Combat History of US Army Tank Battalions in the Pacific in World War II*, Stackpole, Mechanicsburg, 2008

Smith, Robert Ross, *Triumph in the Philippines*, US Army Center of Military History, Washington DC, 1954

Zaloga, Steven, *Tank Battles of the Pacific War 1941–1945*, Concord, Hong Kong, 1995

INDEX

Note: Page locators in **bold** refer to plate captions, pictures and illustrations.